KOREA

GROLIER EDUCATIONAL
SHERMAN TURNPIKE, DANBURY, CONNECTICUT 06816

Published for Grolier Educational
Sherman Turnpike, Danbury, Connecticut
by Marshall Cavendish Books
an imprint of Times Editions Pte Ltd
Times Centre, 1 New Industrial Road, Singapore 536196
Tel: (65) 2848844 Fax: (65) 2854871
Email: te@corp.tpl.com.sg
World Wide Web:
http://www.timesone.com.sg/te

Set ISBN: 0-7172-9099-9
Volume ISBN: 0-7172-9100-6

Library of Congress Cataloging-in-Publication Data
Korea.
p.cm. -- (Fiesta!)
Includes index.
Summary: Describes the festivals of Korea and how they reflect the underlying culture and
traditions of that country.
ISBN 0-7172-9100-6 (hardbound)
1. Festivals -- Korea -- Juvenile literature. 2. Korea -- Social life and customs -- Juvenile literature.
[1. Festivals -- Korea. 2. Holidays -- Korea. 3. Korea -- Social life and customs.]
I. Grolier Educational (Firm) II. Series: Fiesta! (Danbury, Conn.)
GT4886.K6K67 1997
394.269519--DC21
97-5262
CIP
AC

Marshall Cavendish Books Editorial Staff
Editorial Director: Ellen Dupont
Series Designer: Joyce Mason
Crafts devised and created by Susan Moxley
Music arrangements by Harry Boteler
Photographs by Bruce Mackie
Subeditors: Susan Janes, Judy Fovargue
Production: Craig Chubb

For this volume
Editor: Bindu Mathur
Designer: Simon Wilder
Editorial Assistant: Lorien Kite

Printed in Italy

Adult supervision advised for all crafts and recipes
particularly those involving sharp instruments and heat.

CONTENTS

KOREA:

The Korean peninsula holds two different countries, known as North Korea and South Korea. It has over 3,000 small islands around its coastline.

▶ **Shaman** priests use music and dance to perform rituals and ceremonies. Korean Shamanism is the worship of spirits that live in natural places like rivers, lakes, trees, and mountains.

▲ **The Olympic Stadium** in Seoul was home to the successful Olympic Games in 1988. Seoul is the capital of South Korea. The capital of North Korea is called P'yongyang.

▶ **Kimchi** is a popular Korean vegetable dish. It is a mixture of pickled vegetables and spices, and is served as an accompaniment to a meal.

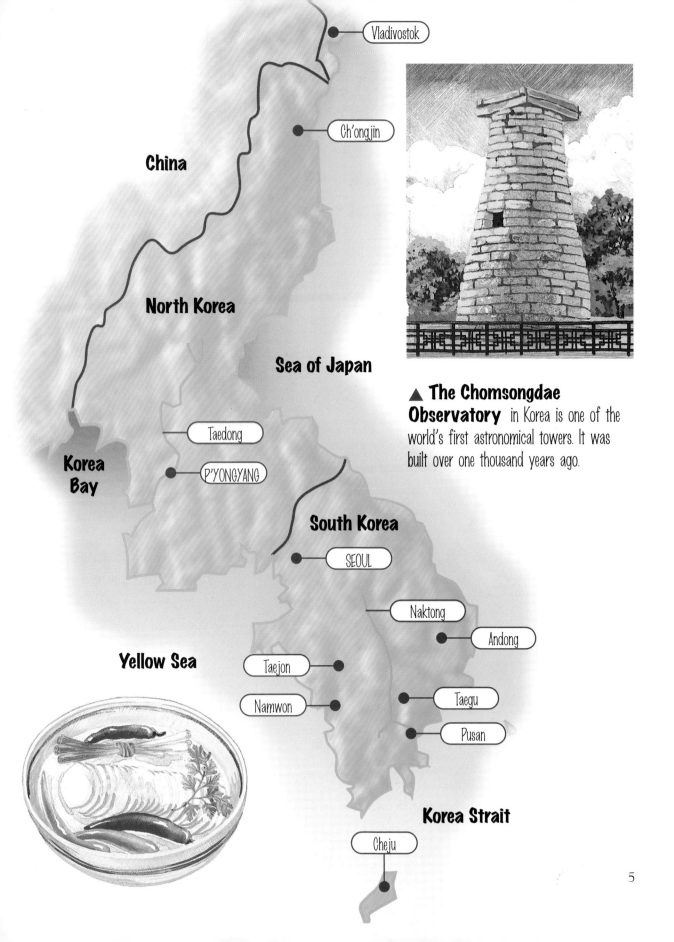

Vladivostok

Ch'ongjin

China

North Korea

Sea of Japan

▲ **The Chomsongdae Observatory** in Korea is one of the world's first astronomical towers. It was built over one thousand years ago.

Taedong

P'YONGYANG

Korea Bay

South Korea

SEOUL

Naktong

Andong

Yellow Sea

Taejon

Taegu

Namwon

Pusan

Korea Strait

Cheju

RELIGIONS

Korea has many different beliefs and customs. The three most important are the ancient religions of Buddhism, Shamanism, and Confucianism.

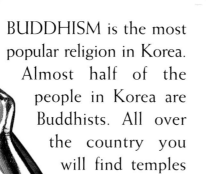

BUDDHISM is the most popular religion in Korea. Almost half of the people in Korea are Buddhists. All over the country you will find temples devoted to the Buddha.

The word "Buddha" means "the enlightened one." Buddhists try to live their lives according to a code of conduct called the Eightfold Path. It includes meditating, or praying, and behaving in a way that doesn't bring harm to others.

SHAMANISM is the worship of nature. People who believe in it think there are spirits living in rocks, trees and rivers. Women shaman priests are called *mudang*, and the men are known as *paksu*. They perform rituals and ceremonies with dancing and chanting. Many of the other religions in Korea are influenced by Shamanism.

This is a statue of Buddha. Figures of Buddha are always found in Buddhist temples.

This is a stone grandfather statue. It is made from black rock found only in Cheju Island in the south of Korea. It is placed at the entrance of villages to ward off evil spirits.

These ribbons are used by Shaman priests to perform ceremonies with special songs and dances called kut. They believe that it is possible to communicate with the spirit world through their ceremonies and rituals.

CONFUCIANISM has a small number of followers in Korea. They study the teachings of a wise Chinese philosopher named Confucius who lived a long time ago. Confucianism places importance on being a good citizen and living in harmony with others.

CHRISTIANITY was brought to Korea about 200 years ago. There are well over 10 million Christians in Korea. They celebrate Christmas and Easter.

GREETINGS FROM **KOREA**

Korea is made up of two different countries. In the south is the Republic of Korea. In the north is the Democratic People's Republic of Korea, or North Korea. The Republic of Korea has about 44 million people. The population of North Korea is 23 million.

Koreans belong to the same ethnic group. They all speak, read, and write the same language. The Korean alphabet is called *Han-gul*.

The woman shown wears a *hanbok*, Korea's traditional dress, and carries her baby in a pouch on her back.

How do you say...

Hello
Annyonghaseyo

Goodbye
Annyonghee-keseyeo

Thank you
Kamsahamnida

Peace
Pyong-Hwa

SOLNAL

Solnal is one of the biggest celebrations in Korea. It marks the first day of the first lunar month in late January or early February. It is a time to spend with the family and pay respects to elders.

Festivities for Solnal begin a few weeks before the actual day. People send greeting cards to friends and family to pass on their greetings for the New Year. Many Koreans make sure to pay any debts so they don't carry any over into the new year.

The night before Solnal people are very busy in the kitchen preparing all the foods for the next day's meal. Korean children try their best to stay awake until past midnight. They believe that if they go to sleep before twelve o'clock, they will wake up next morning with eyebrows that have turned white!

On the following day all the family dresses up in their best traditional clothes. Both boys and girls wear a rainbow-colored *hanbok*. It is a suit made out of silk with a short jacket.

This is a boy's hanbok. It is worn with the black hat shown above. Koreans have been wearing the hanbok for hundreds of years.

When the family is ready, members gather to perform a special memorial rite for their ancestors. The table is

set with offerings in memory of ancestors.

After the ancestor ceremony it is time for the *sebae*, or New Year's bow. Young members of the family must bow in front of their elders. This is to wish them *bok*, or good fortune, for the coming year. It is also a show of respect. They must bow to anyone in the family who is older, even their brothers and sisters. In return for paying their respects, young people receive advice or gifts

of money from older relatives. The money is kept in a small silk purse that is attached to their *hanbok*.

Then it is time for the family to sit at the table and enjoy a great Solnal feast together. One traditional dish for this day is called *ttok-kuk*. It is a kind of

soup made with rice cake in a steaming hot beef broth. Koreans believe that eating this soup is like "eating another year."

Many people also enjoy a type of pancake called *pindaettok*, which is made from mung beans. Other festive foods for Solnal are meat dumplings, sweet rice, and noodles with meat and vegetables.

This is a young girl's hanbok. It has a short jacket and a very long skirt. After they get married, girls wear hanboks with a red skirt and a green jacket.

9

This teapot shows a picture of young Korean girls playing on a seesaw for Solnal.

The folk musicians shown below are performing festive Solnal music and dance in a village.

variety of traditional games and activities.

Seesawing is always popular during Solnal. In the past young girls used to seesaw on New Year's Day. It was the only day they were allowed to see over the high walls around their homes. They used to hop up and down on the see-saw to get a look at the world outside. Now the game is played for fun by both Korean girls and boys. Both players must have very good balance not to fall off!

Adults drink a cold tea, which is called *sujonggwa*. First the tea is brewed, then it is left to chill outside in the cold winter air. Persimmons and pine nuts are then added to the tea.

After their meal families usually spend the afternoon visiting friends and neighbors to wish them well for the coming year.

For Koreans Solnal is also a time to play a

These are sticks used to play the game yut-nori. They are flat on one side and round on the other. The game is popular for Solnal as well as other holidays and festivals.

Solnal is also a day when the skies are filled with kites of all shapes and sizes. There are 70 kinds of kites in Korea. The most common is called a shield kite. It has a distinctive round hole in the middle.

Koreans fly kites on New Year's Day because they believe that any misfortune or bad luck is released up into heaven through the string of their kite.

A game played by the whole family is called *yut-nori*. It is a board game that uses four sticks instead of dice. The sticks are

thrown into the air. You move ahead on the board according to how the sticks land. Families play the game in teams against each other. The winners get to have an extra share of rice cakes!

At Solnal adults drink a type of wine made from rice out of these small ceramic cups.

These figures show two villagers grinding rice into flour for Solnal dishes. The flour is made into rice cakes, which are put in a beef soup.

BUDDHA'S BIRTHDAY

This colorful festival takes place in late April or early May. It is also known as the Feast of Lanterns. The streets are filled with lanterns in celebration of the birth of Buddha.

The birthday of Buddha falls on the eighth day of the fourth lunar month, which is in the spring. Koreans celebrate their devotion to Buddha as well as the coming of the spring.

In the weeks before the actual day brightly colored lanterns are hung in temples and outside homes. They are decorated with special Buddhist symbols. People also write special blessings on the lanterns. They

These statues depict monks who are followers of Buddha. Buddhist monks devote their whole lives to studying the teachings of Buddha.

carry wishes for peace and long life.

Some lanterns are colored bright pink and shaped like a lotus flower. The lotus is a very important symbol to Buddhists. They believe it represents enlightenment.

Millions of people in Korea celebrate the Feast of Lanterns. Buddhists and non-Buddhists all take part in the festivities.

On the day people carry lanterns and candles in processions through the streets. The crowds slowly parade around the town, before making their way to a nearby temple.

When they get to the temple, people take part in special Buddhist rituals and ceremonies. All kinds

This incense holder is made out of celadon, a type of green pottery famous in Korea. Incense is burned in temples for Buddha's Birthday.

PAJON AND DIPPING SAUCE

MAKES 8

1 tbsp soy sauce
½ tbsp vinegar
½ tbsp sunflower oil
½ scallion, finely sliced
½ garlic clove, peeled and crushed
1 tsp sesame seeds
¼ tsp red-pepper flakes
½ cup all-purpose flour
½ tsp salt
2 eggs, lightly beaten
2 tbsp oil, plus extra for cooking
About ⅔ cup milk
2 scallions, cut into 3-in pieces

1 To make the sauce, combine soy sauce, vinegar, oil, half the scallion, garlic, sesame seeds, and pepper flakes; set aside.
2 Sift flour and salt into a bowl. Beat in eggs and oil. Add enough milk to make thin batter. Let stand for 30 minutes.
3 Heat a 7-in skillet. Lightly grease. Add 3 tbsp batter. Tilt pan so bottom is covered. Sprinkle with scallion pieces.
4 Cook 1 minute. Turn over and cook 1 minute. Make 7 more. Serve with dipping sauce.

You can also cut pajon *into square pieces to eat with chopsticks.*

13

POM NA TU RI

Na - ri na - ri kae - na - ri i - beh - tta - da mul - ko - yo

Pyong - ah - ri - tteh chong chong chong pom - na - tu - ri kam - ni - da

Lily, lily, and golden bell.
Pluck it, put it in your bill.
Bunch of chickies,
hop, hop, hop.
Springtime outing,
off they pop.

Drums and gongs can be heard all over the streets of Korea as people celebrate the birth of Buddha.

of different musical instruments are used in the services. You can hear the sounds of bells, gongs, and drums. People chant together and perform special prayers.

People pray to Buddha, asking for his mercy and enlightenment. It is customary for parents to pray on this day for their children to do well at school.

To please Buddha, people make offerings. These may include scented incense, fresh flowers, and pink paper lotuses.

MAKE A LANTERN

This type of lantern can be seen all over Korea on Buddha's Birthday. You can make your own and decorate it with special symbols and patterns.

YOU WILL NEED
Handmade paper or plain white construction paper
Watercolor paints
Scissors
Colored embroidery thread

1 To make this eight-sided lantern, cut out two rectangles and copy the lines as shown above onto each. Decorate with your designs, then cut along the black lines and fold along the dotted red lines. You are now ready to glue the lantern together.

2 Glue the square sections onto the triangular sections as shown below. Do this on both the top and bottom. Next, glue tabs under to join lantern halves. Make two tassels out of embroidery thread.

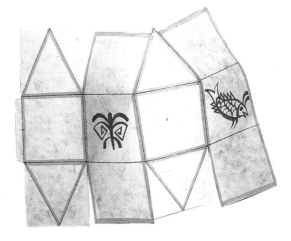

3 Glue two small squares of paper inside the lantern at two points opposite each other on the top rim. Make small holes in the squares and attach the tassels. To hang the lantern, attach a piece of thread to the tassels.

THE DANCING BOY

More than two hundred different folk festivals take place each year in villages all over Korea. Some of these festivals are inspired by legends and stories. This is the story behind one village's dance festival. The villagers dance to remember a young boy who was famous for his dancing talents.

IN A FARAWAY VILLAGE in the south of Korea lived a young boy who was blessed with a talent for dance. Everyone in the village would stop their work to watch him perform his magical steps.

But the young boy was tired of living in the small village. He wanted to travel and see the world. He would spend hours dreaming of seeing new places. He often thought of the riches he could earn from his remarkable dancing talent. He was tired of performing for the villagers for free.

Meanwhile, news of the young boy and his dancing abilities reached the king. The king immediately sent for the boy and offered to pay him a large sum of money to perform at the palace. The young boy was very excited about the king's offer. At once he set out for the palace. The villagers were sad to see him go. Before he left, the elders gave him some words of

advice. "Remember to dance only for pleasure," they warned. "If you dance for greed, your talents will be lost."

As soon as he arrived at the palace, the young boy was given a huge sack of gold and told to perform. The boy grabbed the gold and was about to start his famous dance. But he was unable to move. The sack of gold he received was so heavy that the boy couldn't dance. This angered the king. He took away the gold and sent the boy to jail for life for tricking the palace. The boy spent the rest of his days dreaming of his village, wishing he could dance there once again.

TANO

This holiday is also known as Double Five because it takes place on the fifth day of the fifth lunar month. It is a springtime festival that welcomes the beginning of summer.

In times gone by entire villages celebrated Tano. People dressed up in their best clothes and enjoyed a great feast, with music and traditional mask dance performances.

Women took part in special swinging contests. They would swing on long ropes, and the winner was awarded a gold ring. The men engaged in Korean wrestling, known as *ssirum*. The strongest wrestler was given a bull as a prize. Now millions of Koreans watch ssirum matches on television during the Tano holiday.

Many villages in Korea still celebrate Tano in the same way, however. One village called Kangnung is famous for its five-day Tano festival. A special dance is staged called *nong-ak*. It is a colorful dance set to the music of gongs and drums.

Tano is also a time to drink *chehotang*. It is a nutritious punch made from natural herbs. People believe that if they drink chehotang every day of the summer, they will be less sensitive to the heat.

A hearty fish soup is a part of every Tano menu. It is served along with steamed carp and rice cakes.

MAKE A FAN

In the past Korean kings and queens gave beautifully decorated fans as gifts to their officials for Tano. It was to help them keep cool during the coming summer. Fans are used in Korean theater and dance. This folding fan is called a *hapjukson*. It is usually made with bamboo sticks, but you can easily make your own using popsicle sticks.

YOU WILL NEED

Colored construction paper

Scissors

8 popsicle sticks

Colored embroidery thread

Watercolor paints

Glue

1 Cut a semicircle shape out of paper. Paint with your design.

2 Fold the semicircle like an accordion so you have 16 different sections. This should give you the shape of the fan.

3 Keep the fan folded so it's in the shape of a skinny triangle. Snip off the end point about two and a half inches from the end, as shown on the right.

4 Open up the fan. Cut off the last section along the fold, as shown here.

5 Drill a hole in the end of all of the popsicle sticks. Then glue the popsicle sticks into every second fold of the fan so that one third of the stick is sticking out at the bottom, as shown on the right. Thread through the colored embroidery thread and make a tassel at the end.

CHUSOK

Chusok is a two-day holiday in late September. It is a celebration of the harvest. It is also known as the Harvest Moon Festival or Korean Thanksgiving.

The holiday of Chusok is a time for family gatherings and reunions. All Koreans make the journey home to spend the holiday with their loved ones. Tickets for buses, trains, and planes are sold out for weeks in advance of Chusok as the whole country travels to their family's home. When they arrive, they enjoy many festivities and traditional Korean holiday foods.

In the morning families prepare the table for a service in memory of their ancestors. They use foods that are fresh from the season's harvest. They pile fruits and nuts such as apples, pears, chestnuts, persimmons, and walnuts on individual dishes. All the family get dressed in their best traditional

This is a model of a typical Korean home. Offerings of Korean pears and persimmons are set on the table in memory of ancestors.

KIMCHI

1 Put cabbage in a large bowl. Sprinkle with salt, and leave overnight.

2 Rinse cabbage well. Use your hands to squeeze dry.

3 Ask an adult to finely shred cabbage with sharp knife.

4 Place cabbage, cayenne pepper, garlic, scallions, onion, carrot, and sugar in a large bowl.

5 Peel and finely chop pear. Add to other ingredients.

6 Place a plate that just fits in bowl on top of vegetables and

pear. Put heavy cans on top.

7 Cover with a clean kitchen towel and leave 1 to 2 days before serving.

SERVES 4 TO 6

1 Chinese cabbage, quartered lengthwise

3 tbsp salt

2 tsp cayenne pepper

4 garlic cloves, peeled and crushed

4 scallions, chopped

1 small onion, finely chopped

1 carrot, peeled and finely chopped

1 tbsp sugar

1 large pear

Begin this cabbage pickle several days before you want to eat it.

costumes. They bow together in front of the table in a tribute to their ancestors.

Everyone will then enjoy a great meal. On every Korean table throughout the year is *kimchi*. This is a spicy dish made from pickled vegetables. People used to pickle their vegetables so that they would last through the winter. There are hundreds of different

These tinsel toys are called jegi chagi. Players kick them back and forth and try to keep them in the air.

After their meal is over, the family visits the ancestral graveyard, where they pay respects to relatives who have died with a special ceremony, and make sure that the graves are well looked after.

A typical Chusok dish is *syong-pyon*. Most Koreans think of syong-pyon when they think of Chusok. Syong-pyon are rice cakes shaped like half moons and filled with chestnuts, beans, raisins, or sesame seeds.

This doll is playing a Korean drum called a chang-go. *Groups of girls sing songs at Chusok.*

kinds of kimchi. One of the most common kinds is made from fresh cabbage.

This doll is seen playing a kayagum, *a kind of stringed instrument. There are over 40 different kinds of instruments that are found only in Korea.*

ARIRANG

A - ri - rang, — a - ri - rang, — a - ra - ri - yo. —

A - ri - rang — ko - gae - ro — nom - o - gan - da.

Na - rul po - ri - go ka - shi - nun nim un —

Shim - ni - do - mot - ka - so — pal - py - ong nan - da.

THE ARIRANG HILL
Arirang, arirang, arariyo.
Walking over the
Arirang hill.
Oh my darling, you left
me behind.
Hurting your legs before
one mile.

In the afternoon people visit friends and neighbors. They also play games like tug-of-war, with a long, thick rope. Another Korean game often played during holidays is played using small kick toys called *jegi chagi*. Players pass the toys back and forth by kicking them. They try not to let the toys fall.

Girls play a game named *gang-gang-su-wol-lae*. Groups of girls join hands and stand in a circle. They then

This colorful fan is used in special fan dances performed by groups of young girls.

sing traditional songs and perform a dance under the light of the full moon.

23

THE STORY OF CHUN-HYANG

The Chun-Hyang Festival is held in the town of Namwon in May. It celebrates the romantic story of the young maiden Chun-Hyang. At the festival people act out the story of Chun-Hyang. There are singing contests as well as a Miss Chun-Hyang Beauty contest.

A LONG TIME AGO in the town of Namwon there lived a beautiful young maiden named Chun-Hyang. She came from a simple family that was not very well-to-do.

One sunny spring day Chun-Hyang was taking a walk in town. There she met a handsome young man named Mong-Ryong. When he saw how beautiful Chun-Hyang was, he fell in love. He asked her to marry him at that very moment.

But the young lovers had a terrible problem. Mong-Ryong was the son of a powerful and important judge. He knew his father would never allow him to marry the daughter of a poor family. Left with no choice, the young couple rushed off and married in a secret ceremony.

Soon after, Mong-Ryong received some bad news. His father was called away for some important business. He insisted that Mong-Ryong go with him. Mong-Ryong had to leave his beloved wife in Namwon.

A new judge was appointed to replace Mong-Ryong's father. But the

new judge was an evil man. He saw Chun-Hyang from his window. "Never have I seen such a beautiful girl," he thought to himself. "I must marry her and have her for myself!"

But Chun-Hyang refused to marry such a horrible man. Angered by her refusal, the new judge imprisoned Chun-Hyang in a dark and dirty jail.

He kept her locked up for weeks and threatened to kill her unless she agreed to marry him.

Finally Mong-Ryong heard that Chun-Hyang was in danger. He returned at once to rescue his wife and free her from jail. He punished the evil judge and vowed never to leave his beloved Chun-Hyang again.

HAN-GUL DAY

On October 9 Koreans celebrate their own alphabet. It is a time to take pride in Korean culture and language and remember the great king who invented the alphabet.

Han-gul is the name of the Korean alphabet. It was invented in 1446 by a Korean king named Sejong. He was a very wise man. The people of Korea remember him as King Sejong the Great. It was he who developed Korea's unique alphabet, with the help of many scholars and teachers, who were members of his court.

This screen has a poem written in Han-gul. The type of poem is called a sijo *and has three lines.*

This calligraphy set has special brushes and ink. It is used for writing Han-gul on special scrolls or posters.

26

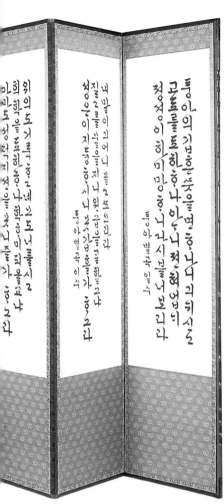

held at King Sejong's tomb. People dress up in beautiful historical costumes. They sing songs and perform dances from the time of King Sejong.

There are a great many writing contests held for Han-gul Day. People all over Korea enter their stories and poems. They hope that their writing will win one of the many prizes. Special calligraphy contests are also held to see who can write the most beautiful Han-gul script.

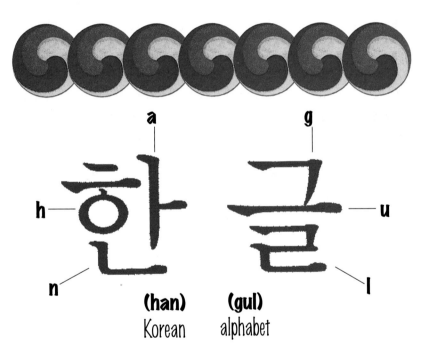

(han) **(gul)**
Korean alphabet

The Han-gul alphabet has 10 vowels and 14 consonants. It is very easy to learn the Korean alphabet. It is read from left to right like English. The Korean language has many unique sounds that are not found in other languages. Almost 70 million people speak Korean.

Until then Koreans had used the Chinese alphabet, which has thousands of different characters, or letters. People found it hard to remember them all. The king hoped that more people would be able to read and write if they had a simpler alphabet.

On Han-gul Day special ceremonies are

ANDONG FOLK FESTIVAL

This festival is held in one of the oldest villages in Korea. People come together for many fun activities and events.

The village of Andong is near the city of Taegu. In October of every year it hosts its famous folk festival.

The Hahoe Mask Dance is the biggest event at the festival. The dance is set to traditional folk music played with Korean instruments.

Mask dancing in Korea is a type of theater. The actors wear masks and use dance to act out a story. Each character is portrayed by a mask. The masks are designed to illustrate each character's personality.

The story told by the Hahoe Mask Dance is a satire about rich and important people. A satirical play is a drama that makes fun of people, showing their faults and weaknesses.

The Hahoe dance was first performed hundreds of years ago. A legend tells how the mask maker

These are two masks from the Hahoe Mask Dance. The one on the left is a character named Punae, a lively and friendly woman. The one on the right is Imae, a silly and clumsy boy.

who made the famous masks had a dream. In the dream a wise old hermit told him to make the Hahoe masks and not to let anyone

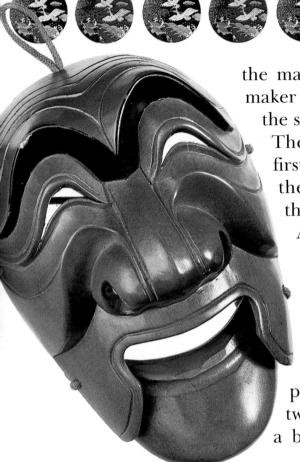

the masks. The mask maker died right on the spot.

The dance was first performed in the memory of the mask maker.

As well as the Hahoe Mask Dance, there are many other activities. A war game called *chajon nori* is played, in which two teams act out a battle and fight to conquer the other team's general.

Another game is *nottari palki*. Young girls bend over in a row to form a human bridge. People take turns crossing over the bridge by walking right on top of the girls' backs. It is a sight to see!

At the Andong folk festival Koreans also take part in traditional wrestling, archery, and swinging.

see them until he was done or s o m e t h i n g terrible would happen. The mask maker did as the wise hermit said. He worked day and night carving the masks and made sure no one entered his workshop. When he was just finishing, his wife peeked into the window and saw

These fans were used by Korean nobility who are portrayed in the Hahoe Mask Dance.

OTHER IMPORTANT FESTIVALS

Korea has a long tradition of lively and colorful village folk festivals. These festivals all celebrate different aspects of Korean history and culture.

Kumsan Ginseng Festival

This is a celebration of the ginseng harvest. It is held in Kumsan, a village near the city of Taejon. Ginseng is a type of herbal root. Many people believe it is good for their health. For the Kumsan Festival people parade with drums, compete in an archery contest, and perform folk dances. The local market sells all kinds of products made with ginseng.

Shilla Cultural Festival

This festival of Shilla culture is held every other year in Kyongju near the city of Taegu. It is a celebration of the ancient Shilla kingdom of Korea. The Shilla kingdom lasted for hundreds of years. It was a peaceful and prosperous time. Many beautiful temples and palaces were built. People pay tribute to the Shilla kingdom by dressing in elaborate traditional Shilla costumes and performing an ancient military dance.

Korean ginseng is shown above.
This is a model of a crown worn by kings during the Shilla kingdom.

WORDS TO KNOW

Ancestor: A relation who lived a long time ago.

Chanting: A type of prayer. Buddhists and Shamanists memorize long prayers and sing the words out loud, often with other people.

Dumpling: A small piece of risen dough cooked by boiling or steaming.

Eightfold path: The eight rules that Buddhists live by.

Ethnic group: A group that is held together by shared customs, language, or nationality.

Gong: A flat, round percussion instrument. It makes a long, ringing sound when hit with a hammer.

Hanbok: A traditional Korean garment, made of brightly colored silk. Hanboks are worn by both men and women.

Hermit: Somebody who lives alone, often in a remote place, and usually for religious reasons.

Incense: A mixture of gum and spice, often shaped into thin sticks or small cones, that gives off a pleasing smell when burned.

Lotus flower: A type of water lily that is a special symbol for Buddhists and Hindus.

Lunar calendar: In this calendar a month is the time between two new moons – about 29 days. Korean festivals are based on the lunar calendar.

Meditate: To sit quietly and concentrate on something, whether an idea, an object, or oneself. Meditation is an essential part of Buddhism.

Monk: A man who devotes his life to his religion and lives in a monastery.

Nobility: The highest ranking group in society.

Scholar: A person of great learning.

Temple: A place of worship. Buddhists worship at temples.

ACKNOWLEDGMENTS

WITH THANKS TO:

Mrs K. T. Dunn, London. The Samsung Group, London.

PHOTOGRAPHS BY:

All photographs by Bruce Mackie except: John Elliott p13(bottom), p21(top). Cover photograph Alain Evrard/Robert Harding Picture Library.

ILLUSTRATIONS BY:

Fiona Saunders title page p4-5, Mountain High Maps ® Copyright © 1993 Digital Wisdom, Inc. p4-5. Tracy Rich p7 John Spencer p17 Robert Shadbolt p25.

SET CONTENTS

LINCOLN SCHOOL